This book is dedicated to Abel's amazing primary nurses,
Roxanne, Maggie, Andrea, Jes, Sydney and Morgan.
Their love and care surpassed all job requirements.
We are so grateful to them.

Special mention to all NICU nurses
who care for the most fragile, delicate and medically complex tiny humans.

You are all superheroes.

What is the NICU?

When babies are born early, have health problems
or a difficult birth, they go to the hospital's NICU.

NICU stands for "Neonatal Intensive Care Unit."

There, babies get around-the-clock care from a team of experts.

- kidshealth.org

I have a neighbor in the NICU;
one who laughs a lot.

She says her name is Scarlett,
and she's an astronaut.

She says all her cords and wires help her get strong.

I know she will blast out of here soon; really, it won't be long.

Sawyer is across the hall.
He winks at me and waves.

He's a really sweet kid
and never misbehaves.

Sawyer, 6 week
NICU stay

He's a firefighter, and
to breathe, he wears a mask.

He tells all his nurses
that he's up for any task.

Maggie, RN

Sawyer, 6 week
NICU stay

Sydney, RN

Down the hall, there's Clara,
a royal beauty queen.

Everyone who enters her room
washes twice to get their
hands extra clean.

I saw a bed rushing through the hall the other day.

Niklaus is a police officer and gave me thumbs up when he passed my way.

Ezra is to my right,
and he's my bestest friend.

He doesn't know what he
wants to do yet. He says,
"It will depend."

The biggest baby here is Brave, a super bodybuilder.

His trainer can't keep up with him. He's surely impressed and thrilled her.

Across the way are Henry
and Harrison; they are
the most athletic twins.

They've gone from two pounds
to five, and celebrated
so many wins.

I've heard Jazzmyree is a culinary master who creates things quite yummy.

She managed to figure out how to get food through a tube in her tummy.

Jazzmyree,
6 months in
the NICU

A really smart kid is Adelaide.
She must be a psychologist.

Nurses line up in her room,
she must have quite
the client list.

Then there's me. I'm Abel!
I've been here quite a while.

When new kids come through,
they pass me a nervous smile.

I tell them to be
brave and strong.

They will grow and go
home before too long.

This time in the NICU
seems long and slow.

Our families wait so patiently
as we heal and grow.

But before we know it, we'll be home with the ones we love.

We'll say goodbye to those who cared for us and thank our God above.

Many of us were born very small, or some of us too early.

No matter the challenges we face, we agree it's been a journey.

My neighbors in the NICU have been great company every day.

Someday soon, I will be home, but I have great friends here while I stay.

On August 26, 2023, Abel passed away suddenly.
He stabilized briefly to say goodbye to
his family, friends, and primary nurses.

He is greatly loved and missed beyond words.

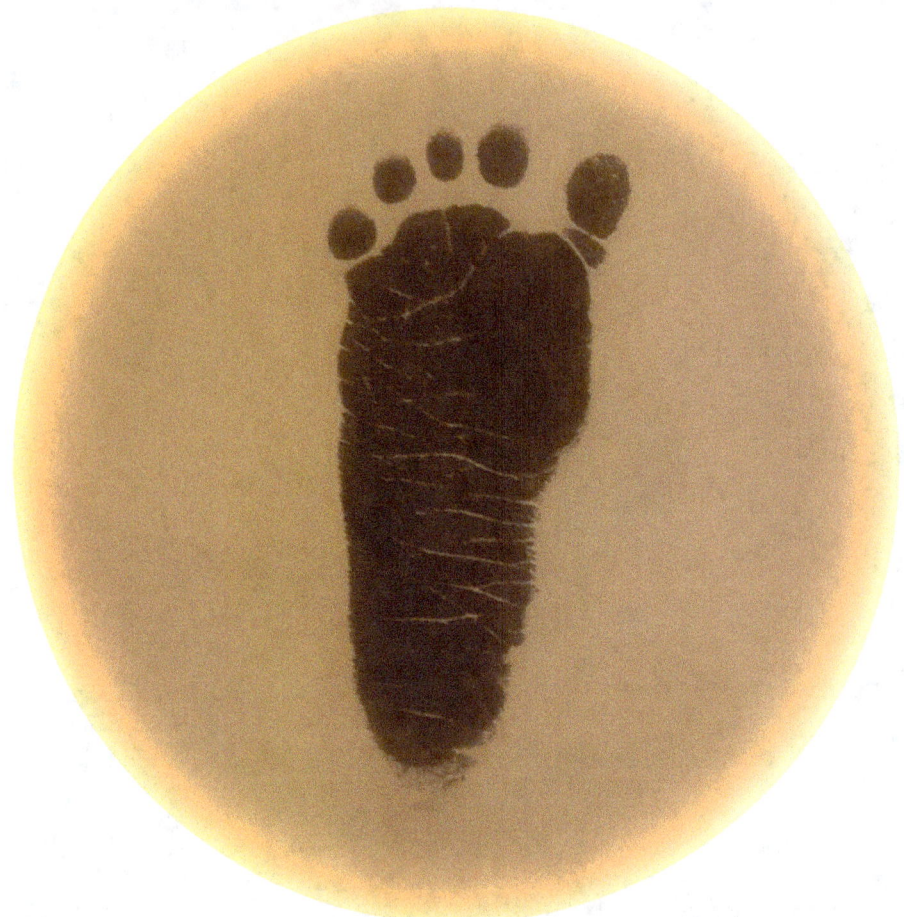

He will continue to live on through his books; inspiring hope, and
showing the worth and love of these amazing children no matter
the limitation or the duration of their beautiful lives.

Also featured

Mary Lynn, 197 days

Anya, 136 days in the NICU

Lainey, 121 days

Rainee & Raiden, 75 days and 87 days

Granger, 117 days

James, 112 days

Vera, 99 days

Palmer, 99 days

Nazareli Michelle, 42 days

Etta, 18 days

Harper and Ryleigh, 105 and 98 days

Logan Grace, 135 days

Evelyn, 115 Days

Charlotte, 121 days and counting

McKinley Belle, 114 days

Lucas and Logan, 30 days and 25 days

Aubery, 128 days

Jaclyn, 130 days

Ava, 87 days

Maelyn, 12 days

Ophelia, 30 days

Ari and Archer, 111 days and 117 days

Brayden Timothy, 151 days

Riley and Willow, 79 and 23 days

Case, 30 days

Taylor, 10.5 months

Jah'siah, 4 months

Gemma, 33 days

Ethan Oliver, 271 days

Grace, 2.5 months

Rowan and Brooks, 33 days and 22 days

Jacob, 49 days

Evan, 18 days

Benjamin, 20 days

Rhea, 34 days

Victory Rose, 6 months

Kayleigh Grace, 2 weeks

NICU Neighbors

```
M P O Q M C A C G W I G Z O L G Z
P H W G Y O Y M J M E T T E Z P E
K A N G A R O O C A R E E C G T Z
O U A J I O X Y R C Q V B A L H J
X B T T S C B P K P G F U N P E S
M R X J P A A R V A U I T Q K R D
O R I F B I Z N G P Y D G I P A H
S W G H S N N Y N A R L R W M P M
P B E F T L F I V U J T T B G I Z
U A S R X A W F P R L K F Z M S D
U D A F R T T H F E T A Y Z V T I
C C C E V I C C G R O T C O D B H
H X O N F P E S R U N X L Y B L L
H A W I A S D N C A D T K L Q S U
A J C C B O M T X L O L F X P B P
X I I U M H F I P W N W Q N K K L
E I M E R P V J I L E P R O L Z T
```

Baby   Cannula   CPAP   Doctor   GTube

Hospital   Kangaroo Care   NICU   Nurse   Premie

Therapist   Trach

Authentic Endeavors Publishing / Book Endeavors
Clarks Summit PA 18411

Copyright © 2023 Illustrated by Emilian Rubio

Formatting by Aljon Inertia

Paperback ISBN: 978-1-955668-86-6

www.BookEndeavors.com

Born Abel Book Series

Watch for the next books in the Born Abel Book Series:

Twas the Night Before Discharge

The Extraordinarily Different Costume Party

How Angels Are Made

The Missing Puzzle Pieces

Trachies, Tubies and Wheelies - Coloring and Activity Book

The SOFT Landing - A Trisomy Awareness Book

Be sure to get your copies of Abel's first 3 books and his workbook:
Available on Amazon.com

Remember:

All proceeds from the Born Abel Book Series go directly to the Born Abel Foundation!

www.ingramcontent.com/pod-product-compliance
Lightning Source LLC
Chambersburg PA
CBHW081011120626
46546CB00010B/3103